IMAGES OF ENGLAND

BURSLEM

IMAGES OF ENGLAND

BURSLEM

THE BURSLEM HISTORY CLUB

Frontispiece: Packhorse Lane, the way out of Burslem in the eighteenth century. This was the road taken by packhorse drovers carrying ware to Liverpool dock en route to the American colonies.

2010 is the 10th Anniversary Year of the Burslem History Club

First published in 2005 by Tempus Publishing

Reprinted in 2010 by
The History Press
The Mill, Brimscombe Port,
Stroud, Gloucestershire, GL5 2QG
www.thehistorypress.co.uk

British Library Cataloguing in Publication Data.
A catalogue record for this book is available from the British Library.

ISBN 978 0 7524 3456 8

Typesetting and origination by Tempus Publishing.
Printed and bound in Great Britain by
Marston Book Services Limited, Didcot

Contents

Above left: From left, back row: Cliff Turner, Mervyn Edwards, Fred Hughes, Bob Adams and Derek Barnard. Front row: Elaine Sutton and Margaret Montgomery.

Above right: Dave Wallett, who sadly passed away before the publication of this book. The Burslem History Club wish to give thanks to the contribution given by him.

Acknowledgements

The two primary sources for the photographs in this book are Stoke-on-Trent City Council and Keele University. In particular the authors are especially grateful for the assistance and time given by Will Max-Leno from Stoke-on-Trent Engineers department, and Helen Burton, curator of the Warrillow Collection at Keele University Library. Thanks also to the Sentinel Publications at Etruria, Stoke-on-Trent, for its contributions.

Other photographs in the book have been chosen from the existing archives of the Burslem History Club and we thank the following for access to their personal collections: Robert Adams and his family, Derek and Pat Barnard, Bernard Frain, Christine Holdcroft, Fred Hughes, Margaret Montgomery, Ewart Morris, Bob Peppiatt, Alec Rushton, Elaine Sutton, Cliff Turner, and Alan and Lois Whitehead.

Thanks also to John West of Burslem Library and Sue Kuzubasoglu and staff at the Haywood City Learning Centre, Burslem, for the meeting and IT facilities provided. Special thanks go to club member Dave Wallett, who gave the authors full access to his splendid collection of photographs and documents, which by themselves are worthy of the publication of a book.

Particular thanks must be extended to Cliff Turner for the time and energy put into this project as the club's IT coordinator.

The following members of the Burslem History Club assert their rights to be acknowledged as co-authors of this book: Robert Adams, Derek Barnard, Mervyn Edwards, Fred Hughes, Margaret Montgomery, Elaine Sutton, Cliff Turner and Dave Wallett.

Foreword

For generations, throughout the region of North Staffordshire and in the city of Stoke-on-Trent, Burslem has been known as the Mother Town of the Potteries. It is the birthplace of Josiah Wedgwood and was the home town of the Edwardian novelist Arnold Bennett, who made the district internationally famous in his celebrated 'Five Towns' novels.

Although its origins probably lie in Saxon times, Burslem is first mentioned as a settlement in the Domesday Book when it was described as an isolated hamlet populated by 'one husbandman and four cottagers'. Not, you would think, an auspicious beginning or a prominent location. Things might have rolled along pleasantly enough for the local peasant farmers, who eked out a hard agricultural living in a community scattered around Burslem's modest Norman parish church, but in the seventeenth century a combination of conditions came together to set its historic future off in a completely different direction.

From the outset, the first anonymous farmers were vexed by poor quality soil that stood thinly upon clayey ground suitable only for grazing hillside sheep and producing scanty brown wheat. A chance piece of luck, however, turned their attention to the ubiquitous and irksome clay with the manufacture and sale of butter containers, which helped to supplement their meagre earnings. Happily, the part-time potters also found that between the layers of red clay lay an abundance of rich seams of fast-burning coal. Put together, these two minerals provided the means to promote an industry. It was about this time that tea became a European craze and the demand for ceramic drinking vessels rocketed overnight. Soon Burslem's primary source of income lay in the production of tableware.

More importantly, regiments of exceptional artists, modellers and ceramic designers poured into Burslem and the surrounding villages, making the Potteries a keystone in the beginning of the new age of industry. Over a relatively short period of 250 years, the greatest international names in ceramics lived, worked and passed through Burslem – the Wedgwoods, naturally, Royal Doulton, Davenport, Wood, Price, Wilkinson and Midwinter being just a few household names whose dinner services, tea-sets and drawing room ceramic art pieces graced the tables of the world's rich and poor alike. And in the pot banks, as the potters call their factories, the graceful talents of Susie Cooper, Charlotte Rhead and Clarice Cliff have burned brightly to remain illuminated long after their times, as their artistic products continue to grow in reputation in the fashionable world of collectables. Proudly, in the twenty-first century the traditions of Burslem's great forerunners are still perpetuated with the modern collectables and the useful ware of Moorcroft, Dudsons, Steelite International and Burleigh, famous names that sit comfortably alongside bold new exponents of modern innovative ceramics with the artistry of Moorland Pottery, Burleigh Ware and Lorna Bailey.

Burslem's history is rich in the world of industry and enterprise and, to the surprise of its tourists and visitors, many of the factories, as well as the grand Victorian civic and recreational buildings, are still to be seen in practical usage. Moreover, Burslem's previous vitality has made it the most written about town in Stoke-on-Trent.

Burslem boasts one of the most active historical societies in Staffordshire, established to continue honouring the town's vitality and heritage. The members of the Burslem History Club have consequently seized the opportunity to compile this book and to share with the general public the results of some of its recent researches. Members are confident that the following images and accompanying text truly reflect the background of an important town of the Industrial Revolution.

As the indigenous trades decline and the traditional crafts and industries move forward in modern transition, the Burslem History Club offers this book as an opportune reminder of another age, a look at yesteryear. The book remembers an important and influential industry and the Burslem History Club pays homage to its distinguished home.

Fred Hughes
Project Coordinator

one

Burslem Town Centre and the Burslem Angel

Burslem's Town Hall of 1857, with a rutted road surface to its side. Civic dignitaries often appeared on the upper part of the Town Hall's portico and spoke to crowds of people in Market Place below.

The demolition of Burslem's Meat Market in 1957. This was a time of regeneration in Burslem, with the Federation Jubilee celebrations following in 1960.

The town garden to the rear of the Town Hall was completed in 1960, the architect being Mischa Black of the Civic Trust. Here the crowds are listening to the band whilst awaiting the official opening.

Above: Prior to the establishment of the Ceramica Heritage Centre in 2003, the site was excavated. Television's *Time Team* were involved in an archaeological dig at the site, discovering that the Ivy House pot works, which at one time belonged to the Wedgwoods, was also located here.

Above: The old Civic Gardens area earned the nickname of 'Pigeon Park' and became dilapidated prior to the opening of the Ceramica Heritage Centre on the site in 2003.

Right: This old Georgian shop frontage stands in Market Place, Burslem. Originally part of Leicester's Chemist, it is now being opened up as 'Emelle' Ladies and Childrens wear.

Opposite above: An aerial view of Burslem from the south. Visible are the Royal Doulton factory centre right, the George Hotel and the Bethel Methodist Chapel in Waterloo Road – both at the centre of the photograph.

Opposite below: The tunnels under the Town Hall lead to the former police lock-ups. The present education rooms belonging to Ceramica are now located in the basement section.

Norris' wine merchants stood next to the covered market in Market Place, Burslem. James Norris (Burslem) Ltd was established in 1879 as a wine and spirit merchants and bottlers of ale and porter.

The Meat Market opened in 1836 for the use of butchers and other provisions dealers. It incorporated 124 booths for these tradesmen. The building's rusticated base was surmounted by iron railings.

The Meat Market was designed in the Classical style and embraced a Doric portico. Arnold Bennett wrote in his *Old Wives' Tale* (1908) that 'Bursley had a majestic edifice… for the sale of dead animals'.

The rear of the Meat Market (the 'Shambles' of Bennett's novels). The Ceramica Heritage Centre now occupies the site, to the east of the old Town Hall.

Opposite above: Queen Street, Burslem, showing on the left the covered market of 1879 and the Wedgwood Institute. Note the barrel hanging outside the Star Inn on the right.

Opposite below: Fountain in St John's Square, *c.* 1960. This handsome drinking fountain was presented by James Maddock, JP, once the vice-chairman of the Staffordshire Potteries Waterworks Company.

Left: A closer look at the fountain in St John's Square. James Maddock presented his fountain to the people of Burslem on 24 August 1881. For many years after, it became a popular gathering point for those who wished to chat whilst in town.

Below: St John's Square, around 1880. Research by the Burslem History Club has failed to determine the function of the curious structure at the foot of the square. There is a clock face on Salt's building, whilst the curious, low-roofed, thatched structure on its right was demolished around 1883.

Left: The Wedgwood Institute celebrates the local contribution of Josiah Wedgwood (1730–1795), master potter, industrial chemist and campaigner for improved communications. Built between 1863 and 1869, the Wedgwood Memorial Institute was a centre for culture in the town, housing a library, art school and technical school.

Below: The Big House in Moorland Road is bedecked in flags for the Coronation in 1953. It was built for Thomas and John Wedgwood (Josiah's cousins) in 1751. The mock Tudor Red Lion was rebuilt in the 1960s and was later the home of international singer Robbie Williams.

Above: Market Place in the 1950s, showing the Leopard Hotel and the very popular Boyce Adams food specialist shop, famed for its organic groceries and the aroma of ground coffee. The shop next to Boyce Adams is now Stitch in Time, a booksellers and dolls' house shop.

Left: Pack Horse Lane was the early transport route from Burslem to the market at Newcastle-under-Lyme and the port of Liverpool. Note the petrol pumps which were privately owned by Alcock's, retailers of electrical goods.

The Queen's Hall is decorated for the Stoke-on-Trent Historical Pageant and Josiah Wedgwood bicentenary celebrations of 19-24 May 1930. A 'Book of Words' accompanied the event and was sold for a shilling.

The Old Fire Station in Burslem stood at the junction of Baddeley Street and Scotia Road from about 1896. The new fire station was opened at the bottom of Hamil Road on 17 May 1956.

Burslem fire station and its fire crew, *c.* 1926. After Federation of the pottery towns in 1910, each fire station had a captain in charge. The first chief officer of Stoke-on-Trent was Fred Bellamy of Burslem station.

Burslem fire crew photographed in 1942. Bill Rogerson is on the extreme left of the front row and Sid Rogerson is on the extreme right. Chief Fire Officer Bob Whitby (seated 4th from the right), has recently passed away aged 103.

The junction of Waterloo Road and Queen Street in 1962. The central building is the fictional Clayhanger printing works in Arnold Bennett's semi-autobiographical *Clayhanger* novel of 1910. Swettenham's was one of Burslem's first supermarkets, whilst the Ritz cinema can be seen in the background.

Georgian town houses and a range of shops can be seen on the right of this photograph from 1956. The buildings in the centre of the row have now been demolished. They included the New Vaults and, just around the corner, the Ram's Head, known locally as the Hole in the Wall.

Looking down Nile Street in 1955 towards Holy Trinity church, which was set in
the grounds of Royal Doulton, which can be seen to its left and right. Holy Trinity
church was built in 1851-52, but by the 1950s was suffering through subsidence and
was finally demolished in 1959. In 1958, the George Hotel (on the left) underwent an
overhaul with the addition of a large banqueting hall and extra bedrooms. Stockton's
tripe factory is seen in the recess on the right-hand side, beyond the traffic lights.

This photograph is taken from outside Holy Trinity church, looking along Nile
Street towards the town centre. The church, as well as the houses in front, were
demolished in the 1950s.

The removal of the Burslem Angel from the roof of the Town Hall in October 1940, after the figure was dislodged and broken in half during strong gales. After repairs, she was re-positioned in January 1941.

Above left: Arnold Bennett's 'Golden Angel' is, in fact, a representation of Nike, a female winged figure representing Victory. She was associated with Athena, a victorious war goddess in classical literature.

Above right: Bob Peppiatt gilding and repairing the Golden Angel at his home in Knypersley. Note the seal of the repair around the figure's midriff. Her restoration was sponsored by the Heath family of Burslem, and Bailey's steeplejacks supervised the restoration of the angel to the top of the building.

Left: The Golden Angel of Burslem was referred to by Arnold Bennett as being 'taller than a man'. She is in fact about five feet six inches tall, apart from the garland she carries, and made from copper by the electrotype process. Here she is seen at ground level, in the company of the Lord Mayor, Cllr W. Austin.

The Golden Angel has often been seen as a symbol of the aspirations of the Burslem people, and she is a prominent feature on top of the Town Hall of 1857, now Ceramica. She had originally been removed in 1998 as part of preparations for the Ceramica museum. Repair work has included a head-to-toe covering of gold leaf and a special coating to protect her against adverse weather conditions.

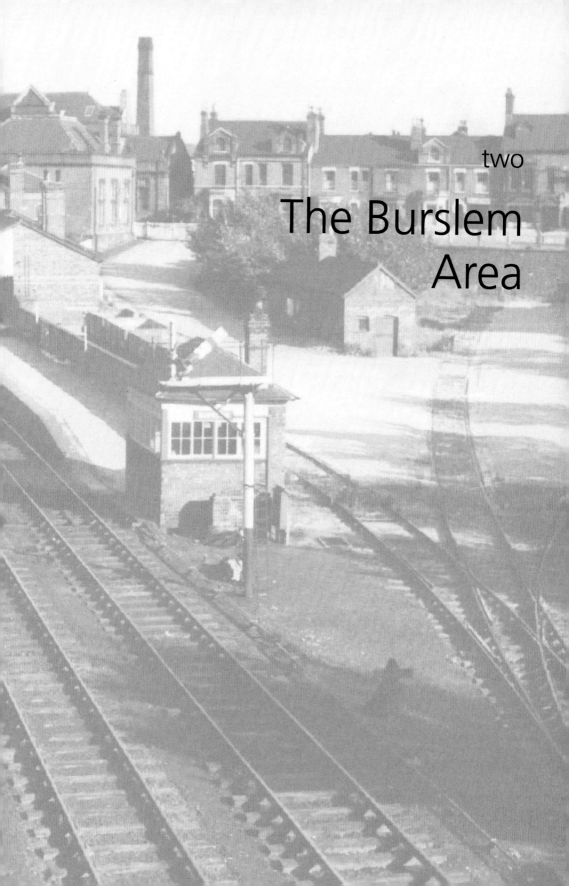

two

The Burslem Area

The Dale Hall area of Newcastle Street, below Burslem town centre. On the right is the Great Britain public house (now demolished), whose near neighbours were the Great Eastern (demolished in 1996) and the still-surviving Travellers' Rest.

Over 26,000 people used the Burslem baths during the first year they were open in 1892. Initially, there were two large baths, sixteen private baths and Turkish baths.

Left: Burslem baths were opened in the 1890s. The red brick and terracotta building stood in Moorland Road, opposite the railway station.

Below: Burslem Snack Bar in Moorland Road was a popular venue for weddings and dances. Pupils at the Moorland Road School enjoyed milkshakes from the café in the 1940s.

The Ceramic City Stompers, who often played in the Snack Bar, in 2004. From left to right:
Ron Pickin (drums), Bob Williams (clarinet), Phil Rhodes (trombone), Mel Hill (trumpet),
Arthur Wood (bass/piano) and Cliff Lee (clarinet).

This view looks up Scotia Road with Greenhead Street (formerly High Street) on the right.
The Overhouse manufactory is in the distance. Today, this site is occupied by a car
valeting service.

Above: Burslem Railway Station, seen here in the rain, was built in 1873 and was on the Potteries Loop Line. The station on the main line was thereafter named Longport as opposed to Burslem.

Below: Burslem Goods Yard. Employees of Parker's Brewery sometimes departed from the station on outings, taking crates of beer with them! The station was still well-used in the 1950s but closed to passengers in 1964.

Above: An atmospheric view of Bourne's Bank, formerly Old Church Street, which was once the southerly route out of Burslem. It became the town's cultural quarter, boasting two cinemas – the Colosseum, 1910 and the Palace, 1913. Both were demolished in the 1960/70s. Little now remains of the thoroughfare.

Below: A photograph of the Port Vale Street area in the 1940s. Visible on the left is a wall-mounted gas lamp and the gas pipes leading to it, as well as cobbled alleyways and steps leading to housing. This area was finally demolished around 1960.

Above: None of the buildings in this 1955 view of Westport Road have survived, being demolished in the 1960s. This was a community known to Burslem people as the 'Sytch', and along this road were public houses such as the Royal Oak and the Nelson.

Below: The Sytch watermill stood in close proximity to the mineral railway which ran through Brownhills. It appears on the 1851 Ordnance Survey map as a corn mill situated just off Liverpool Road (later Westport Road).

Above: Looking along Pitt Street in 1965, with Nile Street running from left to right. The bottle ovens belong to T&R Boote, whilst the Nile Hotel on the left was a flagship hostelry belonging to Parker's Brewery.

Left: Pitt Street, with Nile Street running across and Hobson Street disappearing into the distance. The father of Arnold Bennett was born in one of the cottage houses on the right.

Opposite: The covered walkway linking these two buildings in Pitt Street East bears the legend 'Ansells'. These brewery buildings had once been the headquarters of Parker's Burslem Brewery before the takeover by Ind Coope in 1958. The buildings have all been demolished except for the high building on the right which has been retained in Burslem Conservation Zone. The brewery, which closed in 1972, sold a draught bitter known as 'Parker's Purge'!

The junction of Wycliff Street and Lower Hadderidge. The abandoned Georgian house in a state of disrepair in the centre of the photograph once belonged to Burslem solicitor and historian John Ward (1781–1870).

Opposite above: Furlong Lane, looking towards Middleport, in 1955. This street stood on the old road known as Beeches Lane which ran parallel with Navigation Road.

Opposite below: Woodbank Street with the Mason's Arms public house on the left. To the right is Wycliff Street and in the distance is Povey Street.

Crate-making works with the Burslem branch canal in the foreground. In the distance is the factory skyline of southern Burslem.

Opposite above: The Cobridge toll house on Waterloo Road is pictured in this old photograph taken *c.* 1870. The building on the left was known for many years as Simpson's Soho Pottery. Note the lines of the horse-drawn tramway that ran from Burslem to Hanley. This picture also shows the poor conditions of Potteries roads at the time.

Opposite below: These crate-making works were located at the bottom of Navigation Road, near to the Burslem branch canal. Note the oven kilns used for drying wet wood.

This building on the corner of Blake Street and Hall Street was formerly a corner shop and has a Victorian postbox attached to its wall.

Cottages beyond the White Horse public house in Brownhills Road. Note the ornate door and window surrounds, and the advertisements for cigarettes. Bowerwood Street is seen beyond.

three

Burslem Park

Left: Sally Evans and Joan Rushton are seen here sitting on the Wilkinson fountain basin in Burslem Park in December 1939. The fountains were then in working order!

Left: A view of the rockwork in Burslem Park on 2 August 1939. Gladys Rushton, on the bridge, surveys the view.

Opposite above: Burslem Park lake, *c.* 1957. In the background (left) is Park Road School, now known as Moor Park School. The park pavilion is centre and the aviary is on the right.

Opposite below: A beautiful view of Burslem Park lake in 1960, with Moorland Road in the distance. Most of the lake water disappeared down an old air-shaft in 1921. The ubiquitous spoil tips which defined Stoke-on-Trent can be seen on the horizon.

A winter scene in the 1950s shows the old bird aviary in the centre and a large building on Moorland Road, which was once known as Gibson's Albany Pottery. The aviary was closed in 1995 and has since been demolished.

Opposite above: An empty Burslem Park lake. Recent dredging and renovation work on the park lake necessitated the temporary removal of an abundance of freshwater fish.

Opposite below: Mallard and other species of duck are seen on the ice of Burslem Park lake. In the 1890s, heron visited the park frequently. The park lodge can be seen on the far right.

Above: Burslem Park looking towards the main entrance on Moorland Road. The park was opened in 1894 and was twenty-two acres in extent. The first park superintendent was J. McPhail.

Left: This drinking fountain, situated near to the main park gates in Moorland Road, was donated by Councillor Bowden, the Chairman of the Baths and Parks Construction Committee, in 1894.

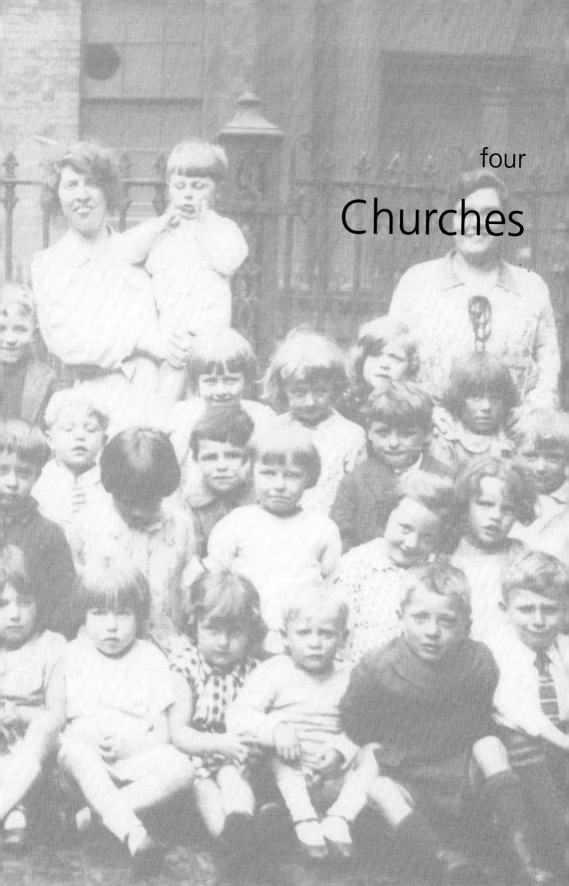

four

Churches

The junction of Waterloo Road and Baptist Street in 1955. This is the probable site of Burslem's first community, mentioned in the Domesday survey. The tall National School building (beyond the car) was built in 1817.

Opposite above: St John's church in Burslem is seen here as it would have looked around 1700. The important Churchyard House, the birthplace of Josiah Wedgwood (1730-1795), and works belonging to the Wedgwood family appear in the foreground. Josiah himself was baptised at St John's.

Opposite below: The churchyard of St John the Baptist measured two acres in extent by 1840, but was enlarged by another acre in 1847. Burial arrangements were eased when Nettlebank Cemetery was opened in 1879. The schoolroom buildings on the right occupy the old site of the Churchyard Works.

Swan Bank Methodist chapel is seen from Market Place with the Sunday school behind. The opening of Arnold Bennett's *Anna of the Five Towns* is set around the schoolyard.

Swan Bank Methodist Chapel still has many very active members who enjoy many and varied activities. Here is the Reverend Brian Kirkpatrick and friends at a charity disco in the 1980s.

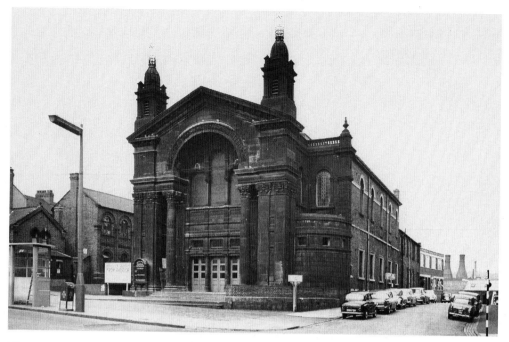

The Central Methodist church overlooked Swan Bank. It was built in 1796 and enlarged in 1816. The portico was added in 1836. The Wesleyan Methodist school and its yard can be seen to the left. The church was demolished around 1970. During the mid-twentieth century Methodist chapels in Burslem greatly outnumbered Anglican establishments and were well supported by the affluent.

The choir associated with Hill Top Methodist church played an important role in raising funds for the church. Burslem had a healthy reputation for choral music.

Among the other clubs and societies associated with Hill Top church over the years was the Hill Top ladies' sewing group.

Hill Top Sunday school in 1931. Many Burslem people remember receiving Sunday school book prizes for good attendance. The annual 'anniversary', involving a parade around local streets, was also popular.

Westport Road with the Hill Works in the distance and the Hill Top Methodist church and Sunday school in the centre. Hill Top church opened in 1837 but only the portico, a Grade II listed structure, survives. The original impressive building was the result of the efforts of radical-minded teachers who broke away from the restrictions placed upon them by the hierarchy at Swan Bank Methodist church and Sunday school.

The splendid interior of Hill Top church is captured in this photograph of the chapel organ. Methodists were famed for their hearty hymn-singing.

The classical façade of Hill Top chapel with eight Ionic columns supporting the imposing portico. The date, 1837, is shown on the plaque on the pediment.

Opposite above: Hill Top chapel and Sunday school. The church was funded by a group of pottery manufacturers, one of whom was the master potter Enoch Wood.

Opposite below: Looking from the steps of Hill Top chapel towards Hill Top school, which has now been demolished. Hackney's, on the right, replaced Alcock's factory, which was demolished in the 1960s.

Above: This interior photograph of Hill Top Methodist Chapel shows rows of pews. Margaret Drabble wrote in her biography of Arnold Bennett in 1974 that, 'if potting was the industry of the [Burslem] district, Methodism was its religion'.

Right: The William Clowes Memorial Methodist church is seen here in 1956. It stood in Church Street, later William Clowes Street. It was demolished shortly after to make way for a car park for the firm of Johnson Matthey.

Left: St Paul's church in Dale Hall was consecrated in 1831. The condition of the church and churchyard had deteriorated by about 1960, and the building was eventually demolished in April 1974 and replaced by a functional, rectangular structure which still serves the area's religious needs. This photograph of the interior of St Paul's gives some idea of the size of what was a very large church; it could accommodate over 2,000 worshippers.

Below: St Paul's choir outside the church. St Paul's was another Potteries church with a fine musical reputation. In the 1840s 'cathedral services' were held here, attended by the respectable families of the neighbourhood.

Right: St Paul's choir inside St Paul's church.

Below: Christ Church on Waterloo Road, Cobridge, was built between 1839-41 and enlarged between 1845-46, the chancel being extended in 1900.

The interior of Christ Church, Cobridge, is pictured here in 1970. The nave was originally built to accommodate 550 persons, which included 360 seatings free.

The Reverend and Mrs Hewitt are pictured here at Christ Church, Cobridge, in the 1930s.

Right: Christ Church's Norman-style font in 1930. The vicarage and church school stood near to the church.

Below: A group of worshippers and officials from the Providence Chapel in Grange Street, Cobridge, are seen here in the 1920s. The trophies were received for a choir competition,

five

Canal Areas

Industrial buildings in Middleport. Factory architecture did not change for decades.

Middleport Park is seen on the extreme left, with calcining ovens in the distance. Burgess Street is in the right distance, with the photograph itself being taken from in front of Middleport Working Men's Club.

Above: Canalside buildings as seen from Milvale Street, formerly Bridge Street.

Left: A large bottle oven belonging to the Price & Kensington pottery factory overlooks the Trent & Mersey Canal in Longport. The canal was completed in 1777.

Canalside buildings at Middleport. Although the canal was often polluted with industrial waste, local people still swam in it.

Pidduck's Bridge leading over the canal to Pidduck Street, with the former Port Vale flour mills on the left-hand side. Note the upper-storey hoist used for lifting goods from narrowboats.

The Middleport Pottery dates from 1888. The partners Burgess and Leigh had started business in Tunstall in the 1850s, moving to the Central Pottery in Burslem in 1862, the nearby Hill Pottery in 1867 and finally to Middleport.

The Middleport Pottery yard was surrounded by workshops used by various departments, including turners and throwers, on what was a compact site.

The Burslem branch canal was secured by an Act of Parliament in 1805. This spur was designed to connect the industrialists of Burslem town centre to the Trent & Mersey Canal.

Opposite above: The Middleport Pottery yard is seen from the Trent & Mersey Canal, with the former hot house chimney visible in the photograph. Cobbled alleyways still exist between the workshops.

Opposite below: An illustration, *c.* 1840, taken from John Ward's 'The Borough of Stoke-upon-Trent' (1843). The coal carts are bringing coal from Enoch Wood's colliery at the Bycars to his Fountain Place Works in Burslem. Hargreaves' 1832 map shows a tramway running the length of Navigation Road from the town to the wharf on the Burslem branch canal.

The model bakery at Newport, belonging to the Burslem Co-operative Society, is depicted in this illustration from 1910.

These delivery vans are seen outside the Newport Bakery, which belonged to the Burslem Co-operative Society in 1922. Dozens of vans distributed bread and cakes around the area.

six

Manufacturing

At one stage Longport House, to the rear of which was the Trent & Mersey Canal, was an academy attended by Arnold Bennett and other Potteries notables.

Opposite above: Note the elegant Georgian doorway of the three-storey Longport House belonging to the Davenport family. Davenport produced earthenware, porcelain and flint glass. Stained glass was produced for a window in St Mark's church, Liverpool.

Opposite below: The three-storey Longport Pottery had a conspicuous frontage incorporating an archway entrance. The bay on the left-hand side of the entrance was used as offices.

Above: Oliver's Mill in Middleport. This has been the subject of a regeneration project in recent years. The buildings are Grade II listed.

Left: Oliver's Mill is located at the southern end of Newport Lane. Flint mills were common in the Potteries. Flint was burned and crushed to produce a fine powder, strengthening and whitening the body of ware.

Opposite: A circular mill building viewed from Westport Road (formerly Liverpool Road) at its junction with Hall Street.

Oliver's Mill was served very well by the nearby Trent & Mersey Canal, on which raw materials and finished ware could be transported.

Opposite: Oliver's Mill ovens as seen from the south. Today, trees obscure the view of the oven on the left.

Oliver's Mill is not the only site in Burslem to boast calcining ovens. There are others on the Acme Marls and Furlong Mills sites.

seven

Housing, Hospitals and Schools

Above: Hill Top Methodist church, factories and dwellings in the 1920s. This aerial photograph shows the junction of Hall Street and Westport Road, with Samuel Alcock's Hill Top Pottery (extreme right foreground) and the Methodist church and Sunday school in the centre.

Left: The back alley of Gordon Street. Cobbled back alleys were popular playing grounds for children from the adjacent houses, including Robert Adams and William Baskeyfield (pictured).

Left: Bob Adams on his bicycle in Gordon Street. There were over forty small shops on the Park Estate at this time. The local Co-op store is visible at the junction with Jackfield Street.

Below: No. 57 Gordon Street, a terraced house on the Park Estate in Burslem. Many of these houses had a small back entry. Gertrude Adams is shown outside the house with her daughter Barbara.

Enoch Street is situated below St John's churchyard and named after Enoch Wood, the master potter who had been churchwarden at St John's and who is also buried in the churchyard.

Opposite above: Brownhills House (or Hall) was built by John Wood, of the Wood family of potters, shortly after purchase of the estate in 1782. The house later become part of Brownhills High School and this photograph shows the adjacent school buildings.

Opposite below: Brownhills House overlooked the Sytch Valley and was once surrounded by a large pond, woods and fields. It was demolished in March 1964.

Detail of an alleyway entrance in Enoch Street, leading towards Pleasant Street. We can see back-to-back houses cheek by jowl with factory premises.

Opposite above: Burgess Street with its terraced houses was situated near to the Middleport Pottery in Port Street. Many of the street's inhabitants would have worked at the pottery.

Opposite below: Waterloo Road, Cobridge, looking towards Burslem. The building on the right opened as the Cobridge Picture Hall in 1916, with Charles Grant as proprietor.

Waterloo Road, Cobridge

Above: A rare photograph of Elder Road, Cobridge, *c.* 1890.

Left: This house at No. 102 Waterloo Road was used as a hospital before the founding of Burslem's first hospital in Moorland Road by Howard and Richard Haywood, who were tile manufacturers at Brownhills.

The former Haywood Hospital in Moorland Road, Burslem, was opened in 1887 and succeeded the premises used in Waterloo Road.

A view of Stanfields Hospital around 1910. It was located in what was then the countryside, barely two miles from the smoky atmosphere of Burslem, giving patients the benefit of fresh air. In 1936, the Haywood Hospital in Burslem was closed in order to open a new hospital in Stanfields.

Left: This mosaic, constructed in art design ceramic tiles, depicts Jesus surrounded by children. It was originally displayed at the Haywood Hospital in Moorland Road, Burslem.

Below: The Haywood Hospital on High Lane was opened in 1930 by the Earl of Harrowby. It was built at a cost of £43,000.

This metalwork design of Florence Nightingale was the work of Gordon Forsyth and was modelled by Bill Roscoe at the Burslem School of Art. It was displayed at the nursing home attached to the Haywood Hospital on High Lane. Forsyth was the eminent Principal of the City of Stoke-on-Trent Schools of Art between 1919 and 1944.

The Cobridge Free School was erected in 1766. It stood at the foot of Sneyd Street and was demolished in 1897, having been purchased by Burslem Town Council.

HAPPY WEDDING DAY FROM JACKFIELD

Erected
1910.

THESE SCHOOLS WERE THE LAST TO BE ERECTED BY
THE BURSLEM EDUCATION COMMITTEE, PREVIOUS
TO THE FEDERATION OF THE POTTERY TOWNS.

COUNCILLOR GEO. WADE   CHAIRMAN,
              T. MITCHELL VICE-CHAIRMAN.

ALDERMAN S. MALKIN   Mrs ALCOCK
COUNCILLOR F. AVERILL   Mr H. T. ARROWSMITH
       "   J. H. BROADHURST   Mr T. W. BENNETT
       "   S. FINNEY   Rev G. B. BARDSLEY
       "   T. S. GREEN   Rev W. BROWN
       "   N. PARKES
       "   D. PORTER   SECRETARY A. T. SHELDON
       "   H. SAUNDERS   TOWN CLERK, ARTHUR ELLIS.
       "   W. E. ROBINSON

A. R. WOOD & SON ARCHITECTS.   Jas GRANT BUILDER

Moorland Road School Lads and Dads in 1970. Lads and Dads football was extremely popular in North Staffordshire.

Opposite above: Jackfield Infants celebrate the wedding of Prince Charles and Diana Spencer in 1981.

Opposite below: Moorland Road School, the last school to be erected by the Burslem Education Committee previous to the Federation of the six pottery towns in 1910.

Moorland Road Senior School staff in 1953. From left, back row: H. Goldstraw, E. Longman, V. Hudson, T. Jones, A.D. Lee, R. Thompson. Front row: N. Alcock, E. Ellis, A.R. Baxter (deputy head), F.W. Till (headmaster), W. Chadwick, F. Cashmore, F. Hall.

Moorland Road School pupils in 1959-60, with trophies for football, swimming and cricket. From left, back row: R. Thompson (teacher), A. Lee (teacher), A. Jenkins (teacher). Middle row: C. Spraggett, J. Richards, A. Oakley. Front row: G. Rigby, D. Heath, F. Rigby.

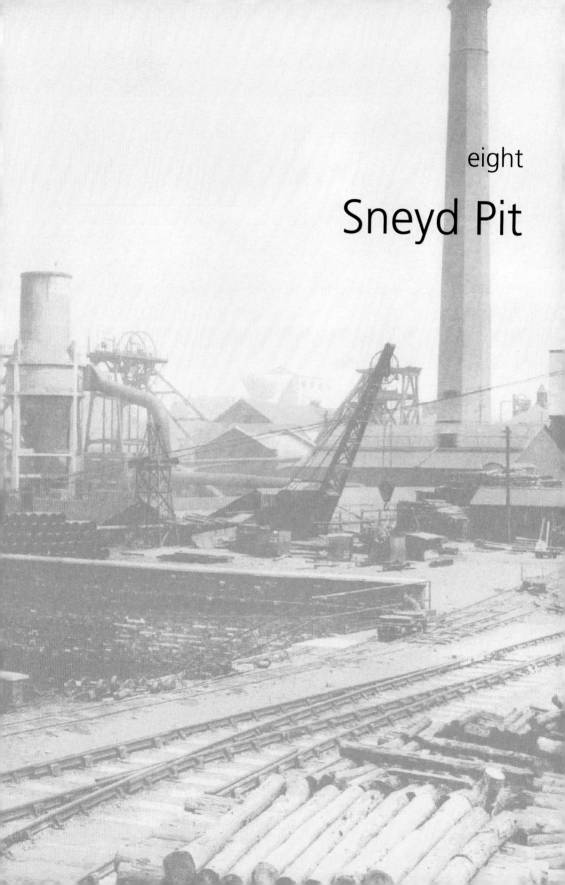

eight

Sneyd Pit

Sneyd Colliery, *c.* 1926. This view looks down on Sneyd Hill/Sandbach Road. Hot Lane runs in front of the terraced houses.

Opposite: Sneyd Colliery, *c.* 1926. Coal mining was taking place in Burslem by the beginning of the fourteenth century. In Georgian times, mining was taking place on the Sneyd Farm estate.

Sneyd Colliery, *c.* 1926. A busy colliery yard is surrounded by an industrial chimney and other buildings. This is now the site of a modern industrial estate.

Opposite above: On New Year's Day 1942, disaster struck at Sneyd Colliery as a result of a great explosion. Fifty-seven men and boys died. This photograph shows members of the rescue team.

Opposite below: Sneyd Colliery No. 2 rescue team. A memorial service for the men and boys who lost their lives in the disaster was held at Hot Lane Methodist church on Tuesday 1 January 2002. The church itself was demolished following a destructive roof fall in 2004.

EVENING SENTINEL, January 2nd, 1942.

Evening Sentinel

No. 24,068   Telephone: Stoke-on-Trent 2381   FRIDAY, JANUARY 2, 1942   (Registered for Transmission as a Newspaper)   THREE-

Hope Abandoned for Missing Men at the Sneyd Colliery

DEATH ROLL OF FIFTY-EIGHT

Recovery Work in Progress

Most unfortunately, all hope has been abandoned of recovering alive any of the men left in No. 4 Pit, Sneyd Collieries, Burslem, following the very serious explosion which occurred yesterday morning.

The death roll is now estimated at 58.

Those lost include Mr. William Cashmore, Under-Manager, son of Mr. Percy Cashmore, manager of Fenton Collieries, Ltd.

There are only two survivors. These were men engaged at the pit bottom at the time of the explosion.

Recovery work is proceeding with a view to ensuring the safety of the affected workings. Two

Mr. H. S. S. Scott and Mr. H. E. Frazer, H.M. Inspectors of Mines, about to descend Sneyd Colliery, where the disaster occurred yesterday; (centre) relatives asking for news, and Mary Belcher greeting her father, a rescue worker.

List of Dead and Missing

Lord Mayor's Fund For Dependents

ASSAULT ON BARDIA

The front page of the *Evening Sentinel* newspaper captured the drama of the pit disaster at Sneyd, including a front-page photograph of anxious wives and children waiting to hear news of their loved ones. Those who perished had lost their lives in the drive to boost wartime coal production.

nine

Leisure, Pubs and Hotels

Burslem Cricket Club pavilion in 1985. St Augustine's, which accommodated the Little Sisters of the Poor, can be seen in the background.

Burslem Cricket Club at Cobridge, pictured here in 1930, was surrounded by industry, including the Racecouse Colliery and the Shelton Iron and Steel works nearby.

Opposite above: Port Vale football club in 1940. The club used to play on this site prior to the Cobridge Athletic Ground being converted into a greyhound track in 1932.

Opposite below: Greyhound racing at Cobridge in the 1980s. In the 1990s the stadium was demolished, making way for a nursing home now called Stadium Court.

Burslem Cricket Club at their Cobridge Stadium ground in 1936.

Opposite above: Burslem Port Vale football team in 1907. The team was formed in the 1870s, turning professional in 1885. The name-change to Port Vale came in 1913.

Opposite below: Sports day organised by Port Vale Football Club at the national sports centre at Lilleshall. Many of these youngsters would have had high hopes of playing for Port Vale.

Above: The former Black Boy public house in Cobridge Road. Late eighteenth century in origin, it was given Grade II listed status in 1972.

Right: These boxers are pictured at a training gym at the Black Boy public house in Cobridge. The building still stands but has long been derelict.

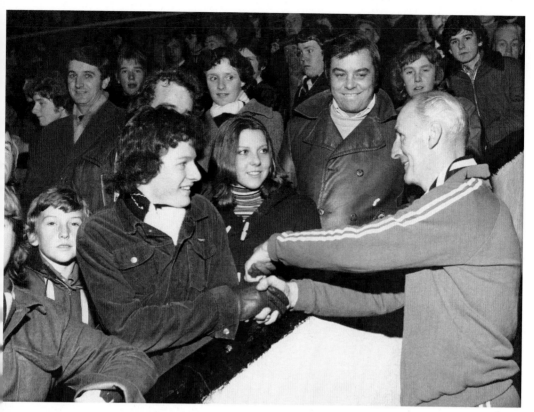

Lol Hamlett's benefit match. Lol was a respected trainer with Port Vale Football Club, situated in Hamil Road.

Burslem Cricket Club last played at Cobridge Road, Cobridge, in 1995. Here is the senior playing squad in that year. In 1996 they moved to their present ground on Greyhound Way.

Burslem Cricket Club players in 1950.

Opposite above: The North Staffordshire & District cricket team (senior A). From left, back row: Doug Billings, John Riley, Neville Foster, Derrick Smith, Alan Coates, David Billingstone. Front row: Terry Harrison, Gordon Follet, John B. Hall, Morris Machin, Derek Hall.

Opposite below: The Royal Express, also known as the 'Jig Post' in Bourne's Bank. The public house, now derelict, stood near to the Palace and Coliseum cinemas. The Royal Express was named after the famous London coach which used the stables here.

Above: The George Hotel was rebuilt in 1928-29. The building's predecessor was well known as the 'Dragon' of Arnold Bennett's novels.

Left: The Castle inn was purchased in 1910 and later fitted up as a memorial institute for returned soldiers after the First World War. Standing on the ladders are traditional window cleaners Jeff Hilditch and Frank Rushton in 1935. Burslem-born Jeff began window cleaning for Frank in 1920/21. In 1928, Frank formed the Burslem and District Master Window Cleaners' Association.

Left: Dog and Partridge ceramic sign. The public house in Hot Lane, Cobridge, closed in 1961. During renovation in the summer of 2004, this ceramic tiled sign was removed.

Below: The Old King and Queen, Sneyd Street. Who would have thought that this was once a public house? A bull-baiting ring could once be found in front of it. The ring survived until at least 1892.

Built by the family of John Riley, an established eighteenth-century Burslem potter, Bank Hall stood on High Lane and later became the home of Burslem Suburban Club which had a fine reputation for crown green bowling.

Opposite above: White Horse, Grant Street. This building originally stood on a major road junction used by the monks of Hulton Abbey, who would walk to their farmlands on Burslem Grange.

Opposite below: The Dolphin Garage was attached to the Dolphin public house in Cobridge. This photograph was probably taken around 1920, as the lady standing in front of the car is Babs Smith who played for Stoke Ladies football team. The Dolphin's landlord was Tom Smith, brother of Captain Smith of the *Titanic*.

Right: Burslem Suburban Club and Institute was formed at No. 81 Dartmouth Avenue in Burslem, but from 1921 to 1986 was based at Bank Hall, built in the 1820s as the home of the Rileys. In 1986 the hall was demolished and the club rebuilt.

Below: Parker's Burslem Brewery Ltd, Pitt Street East, first brewed from around 1860 as Parker & Tyson. In 1949, Parker's, together with their 468 tied public houses, was taken over by Ind Coope & Allsopp Ltd of Burton–on–Trent.

President: A. E. POINTON   *Vice-President:* R. STOCKTON   *Assist. Secretary:* F. BOX   *Secretary:* W. MOULD

Committee :
R. Hall, T. Harrison, V. Turnock, F. Vernon, G. Latham. K. Gee, W. Rushton, A. Challiner, W. Phillips, W. Tierney, H. Lewis

Souvenir Brochure

THE COMPLETE HISTORY & PROGRESS OF THE

Burslem Suburban Club and Institute Ltd.

High Lane, Burslem, Stoke-on-Trent

OFFICIAL OPENING — MONDAY, JANUARY 18th

BY C.I.U. GENERAL SECRETARY, MR. J. B. HOLMES

1906   1971

Affiliated to the Club and Institute Union

ten

People Groups

There were many boys' brigades in North Staffordshire and some of them were even attached to local churches and chapels. Note Burslem's crest at the base of the flags.

Burslem police, including members of the CID, *c.* 1939. In the centre of the front row is Chief Inspector Walter Hobson. Bill Tarpey is in the centre of the second row, with the bowler hat.

Opposite above: Student Prince actors and friends in 1983, pictured at the Queen's Hall in Burslem.

Woolworths girls in 1974 at the George Hotel. Senior supervisor Gladys Bailey had been with the company for twenty-one years when she retired, and staff are seen here celebrating the occasion. F.W. Woolworth & Co. Ltd opened their Burslem branch in September 1929. Its first manager was Mr Hewitt, who superintended the workmen during the last stages of the shop's construction.

Parker's Brewery group in 1931. The barrel was given to an employee as a wedding present, to be used as a wash-day tub! Cooper's assistant Arthur Adams is on the extreme right of the back row, wearing a cap.

Opposite above: Mothers' Union play in 1950 at St Werburgh's church in Hamil Road, now known as Holy Trinity. Gertrude Adams is on the extreme right in the clown's costume.

Opposite below: St John's girl guides in 1920 outside St John's church. Gertrude Adams is on the extreme left holding the flag.

Burslem School of Art was opened in 1907, the architect being A.R. Wood who was also responsible for Tunstall's second Town Hall. Author Arthur Berry was a famous pupil and lecturer here.

Opposite above: Bob Adams on his newly received bicycle in Cow Lane, off Moorland Road. This is now the site of Burslem Northern College. The washing plant of Sneyd Colliery can be seen in the background.

Opposite below: Burslem Suburban Bowling Club, *c.* 1994. Roy Boulton is at the back with enthusiastic young bowlers.

Opposite above: Guild Players, Swan Bank Methodist church, in 1954.

Opposite below: Doulton Ladies swimming club in 1948.

Right: Blake Street, *c.* 1930. Note the traffic-free road, cobbled gutter and blue-brick pavements.

Below: Blake Street links Hall Street and Newcastle Street in Burslem. Parlour shops were at one time common in the town's minor streets.

Burslem Ex-Servicemen's Club, situated at 'Corny Eyes', a well-known Burslem playground adjacent to the Drill Hall in Newcastle Street. This pageant is about to march through the town.

Above: Children in Bycars Field, *c.* 1952. They are: Sybil Keith and Derek Greatbach; Shirley Griffin, the daughter of Les and Joyce (*née* Davenport); Annie Trow, daughter of Alf and Gladys (*née* Davenport); John and Christine Davenport, the children of Wilf and Millie (*née* Burden); Brian Burden, brother of Millie, raised by Wilf and Millie after their mother's death in 1948 when Brian was aged eight.

Left: Dave Wallett and friends in 1985. Jim Morgan, the well-known Potteries photographer, and Dave Wallett are in the back row, with Neville Fisher and Wilf Mountford in front. The occasion is the Beth Johnson Craft Fair at the King's Hall in Stoke. Jim was displaying a number of photographs of the Stoke area.

Employees at Till's Pottery are pictured here around 1923 or 1924. Thomas Till took over the Sytch Pottery in 1850 and the firm operated until 1928. Note the working attire of the group and the flat caps of the men.

Opposite: A family group pictured outside a home in Broad Street (later Evans Street) in Burslem. The blue-brick path was common to many working-class homes.

Opposite: A typical Edwardian photograph of a family posing outside their house in 1906. This is No. 3 Riley Street North. The adults are Rachel and Sampson Price, with baby Gladys. The boy in the cap is William Breeze.

Cobbled back alleys to the rear of No. 25 Broad Street. The older children are Gertie Jones and Arthur Merry, with Eileen Frain and Bill standing in front of them.

A photograph taken in a Burslem studio of Harold and Gladys Price around 1912. The Edwardians had a taste for finery and opulence, and even working-class people were willing to spend hard-earned money on expensive studio photographs.

Above: The dipping house of T&R Boote, Burslem, in the 1920s.

Right: Wilf Davenport at the rear of the houses in Louise Street, 1941/42. The houses in the background are in Dolly's Lane.

Opposite above: The former Liberal Club building still stands in Market Place, Burslem. Here are club members showing off trophies for snooker and billiards competitions, around 1936.

Opposite below: The Royal Doulton figure painting department in 1950.

If you are interested in purchasing other books published by The History Press, or in case you have difficulty finding any of our books in your local bookshop, you can also place orders directly through our website
www.thehistorypress.co.uk